THE LOST ART OF SELLING

15 ESSENTIAL PRINCIPLES FOR CLOSING MORE DEALS - *NOW*

RON D. YOUNTZ

THE LOST ART OF SELLING

15 ESSENTIAL PRINCIPLES
FOR CLOSING MORE DEALS - *NOW*

Charleston, SC
www.PalmettoPublishing.com

The Lost Art of Selling

First Edition

Paperback ISBN: 978-1-63837-988-1

TESTIMONIALS

I was extremely fortunate to have had Mr. Yountz as my Sales Manager over twenty years ago. He taught me to sell using his 15 Principles. When I decided to go into Real Estate sales, I used the Principles and quickly outpaced my competitors. I earned Top Sales awards year after year, and my income exceeded my wildest expectations. Thank you, Mr. Yountz.

—John George,
Senior New Home Sales Executive,
Charlotte, NC

I wish I had read this book years ago. By implementing these 15 Principles, my sales force has reenergized and achieved new standards of success. I would recommend this book to anyone in sales.

—Robert Lyberopoulos,
CFO, Creative Spa Management Inc.,
Scottsdale, AZ

Mr. Yountz impressed me from day one as the best of all sales attributes. His use of his 15 Principles inspired me to up my game and incorporate his plans in my sales approach. His 15 Principles added clarity, and I became faster and smarter in my daily sales routine. My business grew to new levels, and I felt more confident and relaxed.

—Robert Maxson,
Senior Financial Advisor, Merrill Lynch Wealth Management,
Cleveland, OH/Charlotte, NC

I met Ron Yountz twenty years ago when we were both selling for the same company. As we got to know each other, we discussed business, primarily sales. He demonstrated how his sales tactics worked to produce extraordinary results, and the light came on. By embracing his approach, I became more organized and confident in my interaction with my clients and prospects. I still today use his Principles in training my associates. Definitely a game changer.

—Carmen Hunter-White,
Senior Real Estate Advisor and Trainer,
Boise, ID

I was looking for a new business and a new business partner when Mr. Yountz and I found each other. We formed a new business and worked closely together for five years. I was impressed with Mr. Yountz's approach to sales and his overall professionalism. He definitely made a lasting impression, and I still use his Principles today. I was so impressed that I bought his company, and by using his 15 Principles, the company is thriving and growing.

—Todd Taylor,
Owner, Taylor Companies,
Hickory, NC

There are two basic parts to the "How to Sell" process—and the 15 Principles.

First: Homework

Second: The Sales Call

Let's get started!

TABLE OF CONTENTS

INTRODUCTION

Why Did I Write This Book?

In over forty years of sales, I have learned what is most effective in closing sales, much of that the hard way. I consistently observe Sales Professionals committing the sins today that keep them from maximizing their effectiveness and earnings. Today's quote-unquote Sales Training" simply does not teach sales professionals "How to Sell." Even MBA programs at the best business schools, such as Wharton, Harvard, and Yale, never even broach the subject of selling. Selling has become a Lost Art.

How important to an organization is knowing how to sell? In the book *In Search of Excellence*, several CEOs emphasize that selling is critical to the success of any organization and that all employees, from the janitors to the accountants to the machine operators, must be salesmen for the company.

With the explosion of technology, computer-based everything, and social media, salespeople have been led down a path of self-destruction by believing in the constant infusion of an online methodology that simply does not work. You are constantly inundated by emails, texts, tweets, zoom meetings, and social messages that distract you from your productivity and stress you out. Sales training has become based on strategies meant to enhance one's use of technology to gain an advantage in a crowded and inherently technology-dependent market. Sales professionals are spending millions upon millions of dollars to position themselves, but extraordinarily little to complete the sales cycle, maneuver their competitors, and actually close more deals. They believe the more they spend on and depend on technology, the more successful they will be. Good premise, but flawed in so many ways.

This book will hopefully open your eyes to how to actually SELL and to leave your technology-dedicated competitors wondering, "How did I lose that sale?"

The better you can sell, the more money you will make. The content of this book is designed to help you sell better. Selling better is the one thing on which to concentrate.

I am not saying that today's technology is not important and cannot be a vital tool in your toolbox, but I believe it is overrated. By putting more emphasis on developing time-tested sales strategies and less on the computer-based systems that you are being inundated with, you will free up your true sales talents and take your sales career to the next level.

Some of you will assume that the strategies outlined in this book are "old school," passé, and not pertinent today. I submit that the techniques revealed in this book have survived the test of time and are just as viable today as they were decades ago. Napoleon Hill wrote *Think and Grow Rich* in 1960, and now, sixty-plus years later, his book is consistently considered one of the most powerful self-help books. His book continues to change lives today, as it did in 1960. Dale Carnegie wrote *How to Win Friends and Influence People* in 1936. It is still considered one of the most influential books ever written, and his courses are still being taught today. This book could have been written decades ago, but the key formulas for more successful sales strategies are alive and well today.

This book is not for those looking for uplifting inspiration and a feel-good story. This book may feel challenging and like too much work for many. But for those ready to accept the challenge and sacrifice the time and effort required to implement the 15 Principles, you will succeed at the level you deserve for embracing the fundamentals set forth in this book.

I hope you enjoy.

OVERVIEW

What This Book Will *Not* Include:

- Marketing
- Networking
- Social Media
- Time Slotting
- Branding
- Goals
- Databases
- Websites
- Partnering
- Features
- SEO
- Instagram
- Message Boards
- Facebook Pages
- Chat rooms
- Online content
- Blogs
- Motivation
- Etc.

I just read a current example of the emphasis placed on the above topics. I happened to read an in-house training program provided to a company's sales force. Here are the topics:

- Build a Compelling Online Presence with Irresistible Content
- How to Leverage Your Online Presence
- Discover the Best Time to Post on Instagram
- Embracing Technology to Meet Today's Challenges
- Webmasters Can Put You on the Path to Continued Growth
- Five Tips to Boost Your Online Presence

Lots of technology, but no mention of actual Sales Training. Plenty of content and books address the preceding topics. But who is training sales professions to *sell*? Like the title to this book states, selling is a lost art. This book fills the vacuum and focuses on how to sell.

Whether you are in Corporate Sales, Retail, Real Estate, Insurance, Service Industries, Financial Services, Auto sales, etc., this book will help you close more deals NOW.

My 15 Principles, which are time-tested and used by the top sales professions all over the world, will address how to sell. Please take advantage of these Principles, which have been developed by trial and error, hard knocks, setbacks, and ultimately success by me and many sales professionals in many different market segments.

The sales process that I have outlined in this book will hopefully lend you a better understanding of what works and what to avoid in order to close more sales. Once you eliminate the mistakes that seem so basic and replace them with the right approach, you will improve your success tremendously, and more importantly, you will have a huge advantage over your competitors who continue to make the mistakes.

Self-Evaluation

Before you begin to read and hopefully implement the 15 Essential Sales Principles, I would like you to first answer several questions honestly and openly regarding the sales path you have taken.

Many—I mean *many*—have entered the sales orbit only to find it was not the "fit" they were hoping for. There is a direct correlation between successful sales professionals and their burning desire and, more importantly, enthusiasm for their chosen occupation. You will hear a lot about enthusiasm as you move through the book.

A large percentage of first-time sales neophytes fail, usually in the three- to four-month period following their decision to enter the sales profession. The ones that succeed and push through the glass wall and continue to build on their sales careers have the inherent "it" that I will explain.

The self-evaluation starts with *why*. Ask yourself, "Why do I want to be a sales professional? Is it because of the potential for a particularly good income that I can control? Or because of a certain amount of freedom in my daily activities? Or to build a better quality of life for my family? Tenacity for entrepreneurship? Search for work-life balance?" Then ask, "If I do not choose the sales path, what would I do?"

There is no wrong answer. But please, dig deep, and challenge yourself to define why you answered the way you did.

The three- to four-month starting period that I referred to earlier is best illustrated in this example:

Month 1: Excited. A fresh start to a new career. The sky is the limit. Watch out, everyone, I am on my way to the top. No one will out-work me. I'm more than ready for this challenge.

Month 2: Still excited. Fun chasing the business. Love my new career. Starting to realize it may take a little longer than I expected to reach my goals.

Month 3: The excitement is waning. Starting to feel pressure to meet quotas. Self-doubt is creeping in. Not sure I made the right decision. Starting to contemplate what could be next.

Month 4: Not sure I can do this. This is much harder than I thought. I think I should cut bait and take that other job I have been thinking about. Too far in the hole to catch up. I quit.

Sound familiar? This is the classic new-sales-career cycle. The ironic part of this example is that most of the time, people give up or bail out when success is just around the corner. That is why the *why* question and self-evaluation are so important. Only after you've answered the challenging questions and are totally confident that sales is the profession that you were destined to pursue can you overcome the start-up roadblocks with the enthusiasm and self-discipline necessary to break through the glass wall and continue on to a successful career.

Ninety-seven percent of the people who quit too soon are employed by the 3 percent that never gave up.

For those of you that are already in sales, whether you are struggling or moderately or extraordinarily successful, the Sales Principles outlined in this book will take your sales career to an even better place. There is always room to grow and learn new concepts geared to enhance and fine-tune your sales skills. Do not let overconfidence prevent you from attaining even higher success.

The 15 Principles apply whether you are selling business-to-business, retail, or to individuals. Some of the examples will feature one type of sales but will apply to all sales scenarios.

Notes Page

CHAPTER 1

HOMEWORK

Principle #1: Is Knowledge Power?

> Knowledge is not power; it is only potential. Applying that knowledge is power.
>
> —Takeda Shingen

Preparation: "A proceeding, measure, or provision which one prepares for something."

Start with a plan. A plan starts with preparation and information.

This sounds simple and basic, but it is one of the most important and most overlooked imperatives of a successful sales call or sales tactic. Knowing more than your competitors about your potential clients' organizational structure is vital.

Here are some of the macro-overview questions you need to know (I will visit the micro-questions in a later chapter):

- How long have they been in business?
- Where is the corporate office?
- Is the company public or privately held? If public, what is the stock price and stock performance recently?

- Is the company a division of a larger entity?
- How many branch offices, and where are they?
- Is the management considered centralized or decentralized?
- Who are their major competitors?
- Is the company expanding or shrinking?
- Is the company consistently profitable, or has there been volatility?
- Have there been recent mergers, have they bought other companies, or has the company itself been bought or merged?

Questions for Individuals

- What are their long-term plans?
- Is this a family decision, and if so, who would be involved?
- Do they currently have this product or service, or is this new to them?
- Are they entertaining multiple proposals?
- What is their timeline? Urgency?
- What is their budget?
- What are their expectations?
- Who is your competition?

I think you get my drift. Know all the background you can

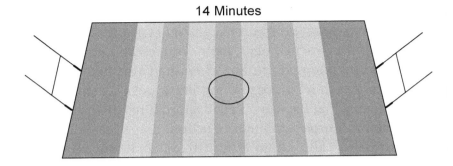

14 Minutes

THE FOURTEEN-MINUTE FOOTBALL GAME

How long is a football game? I am not talking about all the beer commercials, timeouts, halftime shows, instant replays, etc. that stretch a sixty-minute game into a three-hour production that keeps us riveted to our seats as our favorite team battles to bring home a victory.

The first answer is obvious: sixty minutes.

The second answer is not so obvious. It is estimated that the average time of actual action in a sixty-minute football game is fourteen minutes. Think of it—for fourteen minutes of action, we spend over three hours watching and cannot wait for the next game. And NFL football is the most popular sport in our country. And think of this—if you go to a game, a family of four will spend, on average, $400 for tickets, $30 for parking, and $150 for food and beverages, and commit up to eight hours for travel, tailgating, and exit traffic. All to watch fourteen minutes of action.

National Football League teams "prepare" for each game, each with a different opponent, to the ninth degree. The preparation begins as soon as the last game ends and continues right up to game time of the next game. The fifty-three-man roster reserves and a dozen or so coaches and scouts meet to discuss and plan for the next fourteen minutes of action. The usual seven days between games consist of ten-plus-hour days on and off the practice field. Every conceivable situation is reviewed and planned for. So, when the game begins, each player and coach is "prepared" for all the possible situations. It is estimated that the teams spend approximately sixty hours per week for fourteen minutes of action.

Most sales calls range from fifteen to thirty minutes, whether in person or by phone or by some sort of computer driven platform such as Zoom or Skype. You, as the sales professional, have a limited window to start and "close" the sale. The question becomes how much preparation will be needed to be ready to quickly handle the inevitable questions and to overcome the inevitable objections.

The preparation that goes into that quarter- to half-hour call is many times the key factor in closing the deal. How many times have you been in a situation where you are the buyer and the person doing the selling is totally unprepared and stumbles through the call? Sales professionals know the importance of preparing for the call and commit whatever time is required to have all the bases covered prior to entering the game (the call).

Make the most of the leverage you have because of good planning and preparation.

> Prepare (practice) like you've never won.
> Sell (play) like you've never lost.
>
> —Michael Jordan

Your work will speak for itself.
Be prepared.

Principle #1: Notes Page

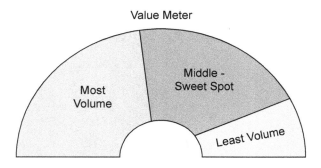

Principle #2: Valuable or Not?

The VALUE METER is an illustration of Sales Potential and ROI (Return on Investment).

Remember: TIME IS MONEY

Where do you want to live? On the left side of the Value Meter or the right? The answer is neither.

Exactly What Is the Value Meter?

The Value Meter can be described as the quantifiable potential market based on volume versus margin. In other words, the larger the market, the lower the margin, and vice versa.

As you see in the illustration, the most potential volume is on the left side of the Value Meter, and the best margins are on the right. The larger the volume, the lower the margins, and the smaller the volume, the larger the margins.

As you see, there are more opportunities on the left side of the Value Meter, but along with that comes more competition, more maintenance, more time invested, and less profit. At the right are fewer competitors and more sophisticated buyers, which means less maintenance and greater profits. I submit to you that the place to be to maximize your potential earnings is in the middle of the Value Meter. Plan your strategy to concentrate on the middle, which provides plenty of opportunity and profitability without the problems of the left or the right.

The dynamics of the first company I founded, Primary Resources Inc., represent a perfect illustration of the Value Meter. Primary Resources was a staffing and recruiting firm specializing in the environmental industry, in which I had a good background. Our primary mission was to augment staffing needs for firms that responded to environmental events and conducted short-term remediation projects. The personnel needed ranged from project managers, field accountants, and health and safety personnel all the way down to basic laborers and heavy equipment operators. All personnel were required to have environmental and hazardous materials training and needed to be versed in the use of PPE, Personal Protective Equipment.

Most environmental firms employed a basic level of manpower only to supplement their core group with contract or temporary employees, which Primary Resources provided.

Where did the Primary Resources personnel fit on the Value Meter, and how did the management and margins of these workers vary?

The management personnel we supplied fit in the middle of the meter. There were fewer of these disciplines needed, but their pay rates and margins were much higher than the basic workers, along with much lower maintenance and turnover issues. The basic workers were on the left side of the Value Meter. They represented more volume but with tighter margins and much greater maintenance.

The right of the Value Meter would have been disciplines such as PhD toxicologists, chemical engineers, CEOs, CFOs, etc. Very few opportunities for placement, but generous margins and little if any maintenance.

Let us look at it a different way. Let us say you are a sales representative, and your territory is Detroit, Michigan. You are selling a standard tangible product that most companies need. You are planning your sales strategy. Using the Value Meter, the options are presented as follows:

The companies with the most opportunities and volume are obviously General Motors, Ford Motors, and Chrysler Motors. You think first, *Man, if I could nail one of those, I would be home free.* But the Value Meter tells you that, although there is tremendous opportunity for volume sales, the margins will be low due to the buying power these firms have. Also, the competition will be fierce, further eroding margins. The maintenance factor will be a problem, as these firms' expectations will be near zero defects. Thus, GM, Ford, and Chrysler fill the left side of the Value Meter.

There are many large to midsized companies in Metro Detroit that do not have the buying power of the Big Three. Although the opportunity and volume are not as great, the result is higher margins, less competition, and less maintenance. These firms comprise the middle of the meter.

Detroit, like most large cities, also has a select group of small but highly profitable and emerging firms. With these firms, the opportunity and volume are the lowest of the meter segments, but they deliver the highest margins and lowest maintenance. These firms occupy the top right of the Value Meter.

The conclusion is that, at the left of the Value Meter, there is more volume, more opportunity with smaller margins, and a lot more work.

At the right of the Value Meter, there is less opportunity, and even though the margins are attractive, the pressure to deliver is magnified, and each opportunity becomes essential to your success.

Therefore, I submit to you that the sweet spot is in the middle of the Value Meter. The strategy becomes emphasizing the middle. It is tempting to look at the pure potential volume on the left and to want to increase your sophistication and move toward the right.

You should study your specific industry and market and determine where in the Value Meter you see the greatest return. It is usually a mix of all three, but understanding the dynamics of the meter will help you make the right decisions for you.

Principle #2: Notes Page

Principle #3: Urgency versus Complacency

One of the most significant components of the overall sales strategy is determining the place in the market your potential client occupies. There are several variables that contribute to defining "market position." By "positioning" your client, you will have a better understanding of your probable success and where your time and effort should be prioritized.

This strategy, "Urgency versus Complacency," is about understanding the client's need for your product or service. Without a need, there is little chance you will make a sale. Even if all your clients need your products or service, the urgency of the need is the critical factor. There are a lot of "tire kickers" out there.

By defining your prospects by the "Urgency Factor," you can clearly determine the optimum opportunities and arrange your plan to tackle the ones that are truly in a buying or changing mode first. The "complacent" prospect may be the largest, with the most potential, but the least likely to add new vendors or make changes.

Most prospects you will find fit somewhere in what I call the "Urgency Meter." Using this tool to measure urgency will save you valuable time and wasted energy and set you free to pursue the prospects that have an urgent or definite need.

Urgency Meter

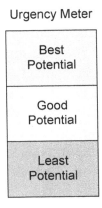

At the top of the "Urgency Meter" are prospects that are either in a fast-track growth spurt or, due to unforeseen circumstances, trying to salvage their business or their organization. These prospects are generally open to anyone and anything that may help keep up with the surging demand or correct the mistakes that landed them in a bad place.

Nationally fast-tracked firms are good examples. Equate those type organizations to the ones you are prospecting in your market. In last week's edition of the *Charlotte Business Journal*, these fast-track businesses were featured:

- National Home Builder Eyes North Charlotte
- Arrival to Add 250 Jobs with Charlotte Micro Factory
- MUFG Exceeds Hiring Targets
- Blue Flame Credit Union Plots $2M HQ Project
- Startup Plans for Rapid Growth As It Closes $3M Round.
- Robinhood to Add Jobs Here

These firms featured last week. More were featured the week before, and more will be featured next week. Therefore, many opportunities with firms can be found in *your* local market. The top of the "Urgency Meter" is a great place to emphasize.

Organizations that are trying to recover and reestablish their former status could be great prospects. You can find these types in your sphere as well. Search your local market for organizations on the "rebound," as they are also at the top of the "Urgency Meter."

NASCAR and American Airlines are examples. Here is a quote from the *Charlotte Business Journal*:

"23XI is investing in a sport that has spent much of the past decade downsizing. Race teams and shops closed, speedways tore out seats, and sponsors reduced their spending or left altogether. TV ratings tumbled, as did ticket sales. The hope is that a rebound is imminent for NASCAR."

The quote continues as follows: "American to bring back parked jets after surge in bookings."

I am sure you can find many examples of organizations ready to "rebound," putting them atop the "Urgency Meter."

In the middle of the "Urgency Meter" are prospects that are in neither a fast growth position nor a recovery situation but are still in need of your products or services, just not as urgently. These middle prospects will listen to you, and if you can deliver what is perceived as a better solution, you have a decent chance of scoring a sale. Look for these types in your world.

At the bottom of the "Urgency Meter" are prospects that are totally complacent and not looking for or entertaining the idea of making any changes. There is just *NO* urgency. The trap is that the decision makers (we will discuss them further in a later chapter) will grant you an audience, go to lunch with you, and keep dangling the carrot that you may at some time be considered for an opportunity. Truth be told, you may as well be fishing in a dry pond, because you are not going to make a sale here. Again, identify these in your local territory.

Here is another way to look at it:

Is it—urgent and important?
This may be an order that must be placed today. You must devote attention to it quickly.

Is it—urgent but not important?
These are not vital to your prospect but still need to be addressed to keep things moving properly.

Is it—not urgent but important?
These things are required and usually repetitive but have no specific daily or monthly deadlines.

Is it—not urgent and not important?
These are items that can be attended to after all the other items have been addressed. Usually, things will aid in visual

appeal and if not addressed can adversely affect the operation.

Your product or service may fit in any of these categories. Not only do you need to assess the urgency, but you need to assess the classification. For example, if you are selling landscaping, it may be classified as not urgent and not important, but it will still need to be addressed, so you adjust the Urgency Meter to match your product or service.

Determine where your product or service fits into your prospect's current needs by using this approach. Using this method, you can quickly rank your prospects from top to bottom.

The Velocity Meter.

However, urgency can change in a nanosecond. Never lose sight of a prospect that is totally complacent. That prospect can become your most urgent prospect based on two factors:

1. So complacent that overconfidence led to not seeing the problems ahead.
2. Unexpected events thrust the prospect into a trouble zone.

Here is an example of sudden urgency: You are a landscaper, AAA Landscaping. You have been attempting to land a new client, XYZ Bank, which has several branch offices. ABC Landscaping has had the contract with XYZ Bank for years and maintains and updates the landscaping for all the branch offices. XYZ Bank is building a new, much-needed branch office building. The building is nearing completion, and furniture has been delivered and employees hired, but the landscaping is not in. It is assumed the landscaping can be completed later. A major grand-opening ceremony with local and state officials, a high school band, media personnel, light snacks and beverages, and promotional items, has been planned for a certain date. There is one problem. No one remembered or knew that a new law in the community required a certain percentage of the cost of the building to be used for landscaping. Without the landscaping, no Certificate of Occupancy (CO) could be issued, and the building could not open. Time was now of the essence to complete the land-scaping in time for the grand opening.

ABC Landscaping has just committed to another large project and cannot meet the deadline required. XYZ bank is "suddenly" in trouble. Here is the opportunity AAA had been hoping for. No urgency one minute turned into intense urgency the next minute.

Velocity Meter

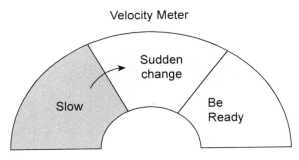

As I was writing this book, an event took place in South Florida that unfortunately illustrates how urgency can change virtually in a nanosecond. The collapse of the condo tower in Surfside, Florida happened six days ago. Products, services, and various resources that were not on the radar six days ago are now urgently needed. Expert personnel, cranes, firefighting equipment, structural engineers, clergy, visas, food and water, PPE, temporary housing, TV personnel, medics, etc., were all needed and responded. Structural Engineers also suddenly needed to audit and examine surrounding structures. You could be a supplier of PPE, and suddenly you are shipping everything in stock. You could be sitting in your office in Tel Aviv, and the next moment, you are on a plane to Miami.

Even if you are not a preferred vendor or the vendor of choice for a particular client, keep the prospect informed and on your radar. You just never know when situations are going to suddenly change. Be ready.

Urgency is not set in stone. It can change in a heartbeat.

Principle #3: Notes Page

Principle #4: Stretch or No Stretch

As stated in the preceding Principle, it is possible for urgency to change quickly, but it is also possible for the demand for your product or service to change very quickly. The changes in demand are caused by many different factors and can be complicated. Although it is important to understand and shift as demand changes, I will keep the dynamics as basic as I can.

If Best Buy drops the price of their big-screen TVs, will more TVs be sold? Yes. This is an example of "ELASTIC" demand. Price will influence the demand curve in this example.

If Walmart drops the price of toilet paper, will more toilet paper be sold? No. Walmart may sell more toilet paper, but their competitors will sell less. The demand for toilet paper is fixed. This is an example of "INELASTIC" demand. The same amount of toilet paper will be sold, but the size of each vendor's piece of the overall pie can shift.

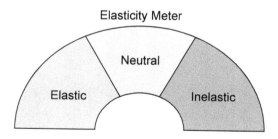

If the product or service has a finite, fixed demand curve, then it is inelastic. If the product or service has an expandable demand curve, then it is elastic.

Where does your product or service fall on the demand curve? Is it elastic or inelastic? How does price influence your demand curve? Can your competitors use demand curve strategies to influence your sales and vice versa?

Understanding elasticity within the overall dynamics of urgency and the sudden change in urgency based on elasticity is crucial to your sales approach.

In summary, a fixed or inelastic demand curve suggests that the goal is to gain a bigger piece of the pie. Competition for the pieces creates movement within the pie, but the pie does not grow larger.

An expandable or elastic demand curve suggests that the overall market for a product or service can grow based on changing dynamics, such as price reductions or things such as increased advertising, easier access, enhancements, education, etc.

Be aware of the dynamics of demand, and incorporate them into your sales strategies.

The Elasticity Meter.

Principle #4: Notes Page

Principle #5: Determining the Decision Maker(s)

One of the biggest and most egregious mistakes I have made in my sales activities was not making damn sure I had properly identified the actual decision maker when making my sales calls and additionally entertaining my prospects. I would like to turn back the clock and recover all the time, effort, and money that I spent on what I thought were the real decision makers, only to find out later that they had little or no authority to sign off on the sale or consummate the deal. The contacts that I had been told or assumed were in charge (based on their titles or the fact my competition was calling on them) were no more than gatekeepers or implementers. They *never* told me that they had no power or authority to buy my service or product. They liked the attention, the entertainment, and the ego stroke that I brought. It was a lesson I committed to remember and not to repeat.

So how does one determine who the actual decision maker is? Also, who are *all* the decision makers? Yes, makers. Let us break it down.

Who would you say is the ultimate decision maker?

If you said the one that writes the check, you would be right. It is what I call the Money Decision Buyer. (You like to get paid, right?) In large and middle-sized organizations, this could be the CFO, if the purchase is large enough and/or has significant impact on the overall composition of the change. Also, in large and middle-sized organizations, middle and senior managers usually have check-writing or approval authority up to a certain level. These managers may have to get approval from managers above them at the CFO level. Identifying and "selling" the Money Buyer can be challenging and time consuming, but critical to closing the deal. Many times, the gatekeepers of the Money Buyers will shield them from unending meetings with vendors. Money Buyers also like to avoid being influenced or placed in conflict of interest. Figuring out the path to securing the "blessing" of the Money Buyer can be dauting but rewarding if achieved.

In small organizations, a quite different composition or chemistry is at play when it comes to identifying the Money Manager. Your prospect could be as small as a husband-and-wife team with no other decision makers, or it could have an exceedingly small management team. Some could be satellite offices of larger entities—you see where this can get complicated, as the buying authority could be local to a limit, then the Corporate or Home Office takes over. Many small prospects are closely held or family owned, all with different visions for how the buying authority should be structured. Make sure you start the conversation regarding the Money Buying authority early in the process so you know how to plan your mission.

Hot Button: recognizes the need and the value.

But does the Money Buyer *use* the service or product? Usually not. So the *user* becomes a Decision Maker. The *user* at some point must be *sold,* or your product or service will never make it to the office of the Money Buyer. The User Buyer, simply put, "uses" what you are selling. If the decision to add or change something the User Buyer is using comes from above the User Buyer, one dynamic is at play. If the User Buyer initiates the need for the addition or the change, another totally different dynamic takes over.

Example number one is when the buying decision comes from outside the User. If the User was not consulted and your product or service replaces what the User was used to and comfortable with, two things could happen. The User Buyer, even if he or she likes the change, will feel insulted and left out and will probably complain about the change and review it as a negative that is hurting the process and should not have replaced that which was working. You, as the salesperson that caused this change, will be vilified and blamed. You must have the User Buyer on board throughout the process.

Example number two is when the User Buyer *asked* for an additional or replacement product or service. In this case the User Buyer becomes the primary buyer, as management above the User Buyer trusts that the User knows what is needed and is acting in the best interest of the organization. When properly sold, the User will sing your praises to the other Buyers and grease the slide for confirmation and ultimately the sale. *Never* discount the User Buyer.

Hot Button: this makes his job easier and produces a better outcome.

OK, but what about the specifications? Who oversees defining the components and specifications that the product or service must meet to deliver the predetermined requirements? This is the Qualification Buyer. This buyer is charged with making sure that the products and services being considered meet and/or exceed the technical requirements set forth by the culture and the goals of the organization. The Qualification Buyer must be informed and comfortable with the specifications, reviews, history, and stability of the vendor and its offerings. The User Buyer is not so concerned about these issues; he or she just wants something that works for them. The Qualifying Buyer makes sure that the organization's core values and reputation will be defended by the buying decision. It is imperative that you cover the bases with the Qualification Buyer and make sure all questions are answered and your product or service is given the green light.

Hot Button: preserve the core values and specifications.

Following this outline means acknowledging that there are multiple decision makers, all of whom must be *sold* and agree. If you do not close the sale on one of the multiple decision makers, you risk not making the sale at all.

It is also important to know that in some cases all three buyers are the same person or a combination of the three. Make sure you have a solid understanding of the various buyers and who they are and have a plan to make sure all three buyers are *sold*.

Principle #5: Notes Page

Principle #6: Psychoanalysis of the Buyer

```
DOCTOR
OF
PSYCHIATRY
```

This sounds heavy, but I will attempt to break it down into simple terms. Each buyer has a different mindset that transcends the transactional components of a buying decision. These various "mindsets" are influenced by many factors, such as the following:

Age
Gender
Time on the job
Job Security
Personal Issues
Family responsibilities
Ambition
Organizational Structure
Decision Making Exposure
Relationships with Vendors
Relationships with other buyers
Marital Status
Political Affiliation
Level of education
Health Status

I think you get the picture. The "mindset" is a complicated array of factors that ultimately influence the decisions the buyer makes. Your product or service becomes secondary to the "mindset" of the buyer (we will discuss this further in an upcoming chapter). Understanding what role and to what degree the various "influencers" play in your buyer's mindset is critical to making the sale. Remember, you are trying to connect, build trust, and outsell your competitors. It would stand to reason that the closer your overall position aligns with the above variables, the better your chance of closing the sale. People gravitate toward others who are like them. Although having a close match on many of the variables improves your odds, there will ultimately be some prevailing buyer mindsets that can eliminate you before you even get started. Let us look at an example.

Example: Telephone Vendor

The CEO of a midsized manufacturing firm has heard enough from disgruntled employees regarding the firm's mobile telephone system. He walks into the Monday morning weekly production meeting, and he is fired up. He turns to the firm's purchasing manager and issues an ultimatum. "Find us a new cellular telephone system, and do it fast. Report back to me in two weeks with your decision."

Scenario #1: The purchasing manager, Jim, is an older gentleman with years with the firm. He is widely respected within the organization and known for making sound decisions; he is not one to rock the boat. He worked quickly and called in four telephone system vendors: AT&T, Verizon, T-Mobile, and Jet Set Rocket Network. All four made very professional presentations and provided their pricing quotations. Jet Set Rocket Network's program was by all measures the best for service with the best price and, therefore, the best value for the firm—if it worked. Jet Set Rocket Network was an upstart firm that very few people knew existed. The choice of purchasing the Jet Set Rocket Network system comes with inherent risks and is not a "safe" choice. Jim, being conservative and wanting to preserve his reputation as a highly accomplished member of the management team, will go with a proven and recognizable vendor. He picks Verizon. It is a safe choice with little chance that his decision will be challenged or disputed. His esteem within the organization is protected. But was it the best choice?

In this example, the Jet Set Rocket Network salesperson never had a chance to make the sale. The product itself and the price and ultimate best value for the organization did not matter. The mindset of the buyer dictated that only a "safe" option could be entertained.

Scenario #2: Same situation but the purchasing manager, John, is a late-twenties, overly ambitious, very energetic go-getter. He is a risk taker, greatly confident in his abilities, and not totally committed to a long-term employment situation with this organization. He interviews the same cell phone vendors. He picks Jet Set Rocket Network, knowing that very few have even heard of this company and knowing, if it does not work, he will be viewed as a possible liability to the organization and that his job may be in jeopardy. His thought process is that if it does work out, he will be seen as a somewhat forward-thinking manager with skills that will greatly impact the success of the organization. His status and exposure within the organization will be enhanced, and he will most likely be promoted. His mindset also takes into consideration what happens if his decision is a total failure. He believes he can find another, possibly better, career quickly. He is so confident that either result will be a win for him. AT&T, Verizon, and T-Mobile never had a chance. The product did not matter.

The complicated variables that comprise the Buyer's mindset most likely will determine his or her buying decision more than the overall value of the product or service being sold. It then becomes imperative that you, the salesperson, dive deeply into understanding the variable aspects of your buyers' total profile and know your position so you can hopefully overcome any mismatches and create a psychological victory for the buyer.

The end game is to build *TRUST*. Once your prospect trusts you, you are 90 percent of the way to the sale.

Principle #6: Notes Page

Principle #7: What Are You Selling?

As we learned in the preceding chapter, the mindset or the psyche of the buyer outweighs in many ways the product or the service being sold. This chapter is about understanding what your clients are seeking from a personal standpoint. Yes, personal standpoint. It is true that some buyers are "company men or women" and will always put the organization first in their buying decisions. But I submit to you that these buyers are in not only the minority but an extremely small minority. Most buyers, whether mom-and-pop or large conglomeration, are consciously or subconsciously needing a "fix" for their psyche. These buyers comprise a huge majority.

Your emphasis must be on creating a "fix" for the buyers' psyche, not on the product or service.

If you buy a bottle of perfume or cologne, what are you buying? A bottle of colored water? No. You are buying romance, sex, attention, etc. The product inside the bottle has nothing to do with *what* you are buying. You are buying a fix for the psyche.

As discussed in the previous chapter, each buyer has a unique set of characteristics and circumstances that lead to his or her "fix," which will produce a benefit and fill a need. Some buyers are simply lonely and introverted and need a friend, so focus on establishing a sincere and true friendship; that "fix" will lead to more sales than if you focus on the product or service. Some buyers are very conservative and do not want to rock the boat. Remember the conservative buyer for the cell phone system. The "fix" is to go overboard in reassuring these buyers that your product or service has been tested and peer reviewed and will absolutely be seen as a "safe" choice, as opposed to touting the features and/or pricing. Focus on the psyche.

Some buyers have relationships with other vendors. This situation is common and sometimes difficult to overcome. Finding the "fix" means not only establishing a good relationship with the buyer but repositioning the competition. In the book *Positioning* by Al Ries and Jack Trout (one of my favorite business-related reads), the methods of "repositioning" competitors are outlined, and many examples are used to demonstrate the effectiveness of making buyers see their vendors in a different light. One example I like is when Pepsi used the slogan "The choice of a new generation." Obviously, Pepsi was attempting to paint Coke as old-fashioned and passé. You can do the same when your prospect has close relationships with other vendors; figure out a subtle way to change their perception of those established vendors. Be creative, and you will have a good shot at the "fix" without pushing *your* product or service.

Some buyers have just been assigned the role of "buyer" and have little or no experience in their new position. They can be intimidated by the added responsibility and may be hesitant to pull the trigger. Also, when news of the change hits the street, competitors will come flocking to get in the door with the new buyer. The psyche of the new buyer is one of insecurity and caution; they do not want to be taken advantage of. The "fix" in this scenario is to make the new buyer feel comfortable and confident. The best approach is counterintuitive. The first impulse for most vendors is to rush to the scene, trying to be first and get a leg up on the competition. I believe this approach would tend to exacerbate the psyche of the new buyer and add confusion and nervousness to the mix. The buyer needs time to settle in and gain a little footing without feeling pressured to make decisions quickly. I say let the dust settle. Avoid the "rush to the line" of your competitors. When you feel the time is right, approach the new buyer in a calm, no-pressure, friendly manner. You will stand out and make an impression on the new buyer as someone who can be trusted to give the best advice and has their best interest at heart. Many times, being last to the party makes the best impression.

Some buyers have tremendous family responsibilities and feel pulled in many directions. These buyers find it hard to stay focused and have feelings of guilt that they are giving their all to neither their job nor their family. Their psyche is one of feeling inadequate and ineffectual. They feel as if they are underproductive at work and deficient at home. Attend soccer game or finish report? These buyers are sincere and genuinely care about their jobs and their families, but finding the right balance is frustrating. They need emotional support, positive feedback, and confirmation that they are actually doing better than they think. Here is a great opportunity to provide the moral and personal support that will truly and sincerely connect with the buyer. Talk about your own similar situations and stress that the buyer is not the lone ranger—that many face the same challenges. Again, understanding and helping "fix" the psyche is the key to hopefully making the sale. The product or service will not "fix" the psyche. *What* you are selling is the "fix."

There are many more examples of buyers' psyche that I could use, but I think you get the picture. *What* you can do up front with each prospect is determine, the best you can, the psyche, and design an action plan that will match and, in some cases, help the buyer. If you understand the underlying issues that influence the buyer's decisions and develop an approach that will lead to a "fix," you will be miles ahead of the game. At that point, your product or service will look like a winner to the buyer.

Again, *trust* will get you there.

Principle #7: Notes Page

CHAPTER 2

THE SALES CALL

Principle #8: No Vision

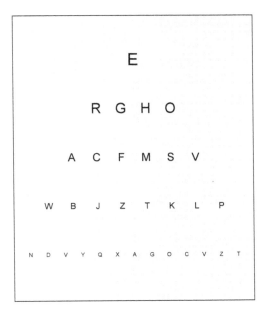

Things that are visible are brief and fleeting, while things that are invisible are everlasting.

—Ephesians 3:20

Now that we have established the processes for determining priorities and understanding buyers' true motivators, it is time to move to the next segment, which will focus on the sales call itself.

Before COVID-19, the traditional sales call was in person. In today's world, both in-person and some versions of Zoom are sales calls. In both cases, the timing of visuals is critical. Let us start with the traditional in-person call.

I am about to discuss one of my Top Ten pet peeves and one of the biggest mistakes sales professionals make on a sales call. This mistake is made on 90 percent of sales calls that I have witnessed. The mistake is so common that one can almost expect it. Only sales professionals that have been taught how not to make this mistake will correctly turn a huge disadvantage into a huge advantage. Are you now anxious to know what the mistake is? That is how anxious your prospect will be for you to reveal what you have been holding back.

The mistake is the timing involved in presenting any printed materials, brochures, visual aids, proposals, etc. Most sales professionals will, upon beginning the sales call, immediately present to the prospect brochures that are available. Why is this a mistake? Once the prospect has the brochure and/or other printed materials, he or she immediately begins looking at the material. The prospect is now no longer focused on what you have to say but is interested in perusing the slick marketing material you have prematurely delivered. You now have less than the prospect's full attention. Your sales skills have been compromised. You might as well have left the room.

So, what is the right approach? The right approach is so powerful that it enhances how bad the wrong approach is. By presenting the brochures at the right time, you can not only control the prospect's attention but affect the prospect's curiosity to the point that the prospect is anxiously waiting to see what you have been holding back. It is a powerful tactic. The correct way to present your visuals is to have them in your hands but not present them until late in the call. The prospect will be tuned in to your every word. You will be able to probe, ask your questions, decide what is important, determine what to emphasize, and use your sales skills to the maximum. Then, and only then, you can present the marketing material and point out the areas of special concern and interest to your prospect.

Look at it this way. We all love a great mystery movie, one that keeps you guessing and focused until the very end. Only at the end is the mystery answered—and usually with a "twist" that no one expected. If the answer had been revealed at the beginning of the movie, you would have lost both interest and focus. By holding back the answer, the movie keeps you involved and anxious to find out just what will be revealed in the end. This example is analogous to the timing of the visuals in the sales call.

The same method can be used in a Zoom call. By keeping charts or pictures in your background and a little out of focus, you can achieve the same effect as an in-person call. Toward the end, bring the visuals into focus and emphasize the features that match your prospect's needs. (We will discuss this more later in the book.)

By not making the mistake of revealing the visuals up front, you have kept your prospect's attention and increased your odds of making the sale.

Principle #8: Notes Page

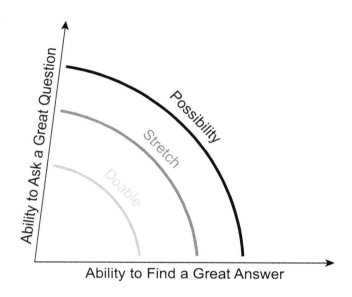

Principle #9: Ask and You Shall Receive

You are now in control of the sales call. Your prospect is itching to see what you are withholding. Now is the time to establish needs and other hot-button reasons that will guide you to match your product or service to your prospect's overall situation.

I had a big corporate sales job many years ago. I was living in Raleigh, NC at the time. My employer dictated that all National Account Sales Reps wear a suit every day. Not slacks and a sport coat, but a suit. Therefore, I needed several really nice suits. Needing a new suit, I went to one of Raleigh's finest men's stores to look for a new suit. As soon as I entered, an overly aggressive sales representative met me. He did ask one good question: "What can I help you with today?"

That was the last thing he did right. I replied that I was looking for a new suit. He said, "OK, you look like about a 36 regular." (I have grown since then.) And he immediately led me to the 36 regular rack, pulled out a gray suit that he said would look great on me, and started to lead me to the dressing room. He continued to stress how great this suit would work for me. There was a slight problem. I already owned the very suit he was pushing on me. I was looking for a *blue* suit. He would never have sold me that gray suit, no matter how hard he tried. I did not *need* a gray suit. He failed to ask the questions that would reveal what I needed. He had immediately started to *sell* me on something I would never buy. By slowing down, asking a few more questions, and letting me talk, he might have made a sale. I left the store and bought a *blue* suit down the street at his competitor. Sure, I could have stuck with this guy and looked at his *blue* suits, but I felt his approach was too pushy and really a waste of my time.

Obviously, he had not been trained to SELL. Too bad, because he lost a sale, the store lost a sale, and there would be no referrals. Amazing what a difference some basic training on how to sell would have made.

Establishing needs, timing (urgency), mindset, how to get other buyers involved, budgets, new or existing products or services, what specifications are required, overall expectations, etc.—all require one thing. Asking questions. By asking questions, you get the prospect talking. You are making him or her feel important. And subconsciously, in many cases, the prospect sells him- or herself. By allowing the prospect to reveal the many factors influencing the buying decisions, you arm yourself with the knowledge you need to close the deal. Most of the time, they just want to be heard and have their concerns recognized.

Engaging in meaningful conversation with your prospects will make all the difference.

Reflecting on the suit story: a soft greeting and a series of questions would have made a big difference. He would have engaged me to the point that I just might have sold myself.

In any event, the salesman or woman would now be armed with the knowledge that would lead to a probable sale, one that I would feel excited about and in which I would participate. There is another benefit that the salesperson would more than likely gain, a repeat sale. Based on the great experience I had, I would more than likely go back to the same store and to the same salesperson for my next suit. But hold on. There is another benefit to be gained by the salesperson. Referrals. The lifeblood of all professional salesmen and women. I know many contemporaries that need suits. Where do you think I would send them?

A long-running misconception is that the gift of gab is essential to being a great salesperson, along with an outgoing personality. It is not about the gift of gab, but about a complex mixture of personal traits driven by the desire and enthusiasm that translates to salesmanship. Some of the best salespeople I know are on the quiet side. They know that getting the prospect to talk is the key. Therefore, they ask the right questions and listen intently to the answers. The listeners, not the gabbers, have the upper hand. The listeners understand how important it is to get the prospect talking. In most cases, the prospect really does not care about hearing about you. The prospect wants *you* to know about *them*.

Here is a great example of a sales approach that not only incorporates asking questions but demonstrates the power of not starting with a sales pitch. It requires uncovering what is going on in the prospect's life and what is genuinely important so that you address what they feel is most important.

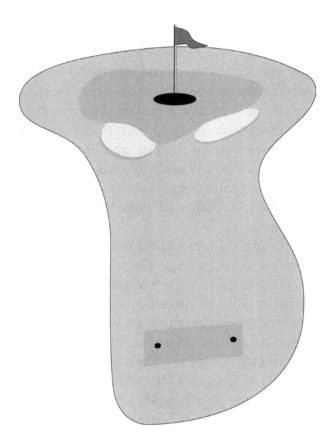

There was a fairly accomplished professional golfer, not great but rather good. He had won a few PGA tournaments and had been close in a couple of majors. He was entering his late thirties and was suddenly struggling with his swing. He had reached out to a couple of swing coaches, but they had been unable to "fix" his swing. He was precariously close to losing his tour card and not being able to compete in tournaments. He decided to hire one of the most famous swing coaches out of desperation. This coach's hourly fee was awfully expensive.

The golfer got to the practice range early on the day of his swing lesson and was hitting a few balls when the swing coach arrived. They greeted each other, and the golfer thought they would start analyzing his swing. Instead, the swing coach said, "Let's go up to the clubhouse and get a Coke and talk for a while." The golfer just about went ballistic. He said, "I'm paying you big bucks, and I am about to lose my tour card, and you want to go get a Coke. Are you crazy?"

They went to the clubhouse and sat down with a Coke, and the swing coach started asking questions, all unrelated to the golf swing. He wanted to know what was going on in the golfer's life outside of golf. He wanted to understand his mind-set and current life situation—marriage issues, kids, money, health, etc. By asking these questions, he accomplished two things: 1) he better understood how to approach the swing lessons, in that he knew where to focus and how to better communicate, and 2) he built a relationship, so to speak, and earned the golfer's trust.

Asking questions, the right questions, is the foundation for the series of events that will follow to build trust and accomplish the goal. The golfer, by the way, was able to approach his swing lessons with a more trusting and open-minded attitude. He kept his tour card and went on to compete on the Tour once again. And you bet he referred the swing coach.

An Emotional Connection Deepens Trust and Accelerates Conversion.

Asking the right questions at the right times is easy to master and produces sales, repeat sales, and referrals—a trifecta winning ticket. Put this strategy in your quiver and use it whenever you can.

Principle #9: Notes Page

Principle #10: You Are Not a Volunteer

Unless you live in Tennessee or matriculated at the University of Tennessee at Knoxville, you are *not* a volunteer. And even if you are a Tennessee Volunteer, you will *not* be a volunteer when it comes to sales calls. We discussed at length in the preceding chapter asking the right questions at the right times. So how do you frame the questions, and how do you respond? *You* are in control of the question and answer. However, the prospect will certainly ask questions directed at you. *How* you answer the questions posed to you is another critical part of the sales call. There is one and only one right way to answer questions from the prospect.

The right answer is to answer the question in the most succinct manner, not straying beyond the basic response. Answer the question and—excuse my French—shut up. Volunteering additional information that has not been asked for can be the final nail in the coffin. By volunteering information, you are likely to say something the prospect disagrees with, had a bad experience with, does not like, or finds adverse to his or her psyche. It could be as simple as praising a brand with which he or she has a problem or a sports team that he or she hates.

As my company, Primary Resources Inc., started to grow, our office telephone system became overburdened, and an updated, larger system was needed to support our growth. I selected three telephone system vendors and asked them to present their equipment and their pricing. All three made the mistake of immediately handing me their brochures (no vision) and espousing the features and benefits of their systems without asking *what* was most important to me (ask and you shall receive). I narrowed down the choices and was ready to select the vendor I thought best fit our needs. When that vendor returned for the follow-up call, I was ready to sign the purchase agreement, until something unnecessary and not critical to my decision popped up. As we were going over the details of the purchase, the vendor's sales representative began volunteering additional information about the system and her company that I had not asked about and did not need. The straw that broke the camel's back was when she showed me a brochure that revealed that a certain bank was providing financial backing for her company. She wrongly assumed that I would be impressed and that the connection to the large and well-known bank would further seal the deal.

Little did she know that, when I started Primary Resources, I went to the same bank she was touting, which also happened to be my bank. I had been with that bank for many years. I applied for a business loan from my bank to help with startup costs. I was turned down. I walked out of the bank in disbelief, because I had already committed to starting the company and was shocked that I could not get the loan. Right across the street was a branch of my bank's competitor. I had never done any business there. I walked across the street, still a little shaken, and entered the bank. I asked to see a business loan officer, and a few minutes later, I was in the loan officer's office presenting my case. In less than thirty minutes, I had my loan. I decided right then and there never to do business with my old bank again. That experience was still fresh in my mind when the sales representative volunteered the connection between her company and that bank. Maybe I overreacted, but I stopped the appointment immediately. I thanked the sales representative for her time and effort and told her I was going to further think things through. I called in my second choice, and we struck a deal.

My first choice lost the sale by volunteering information that was simply not needed and potentially a deal breaker. Volunteering product or service information, or even personal unrelated expressions, can seriously affect the outcome.

Attorneys stress to their clients who are testifying or being deposed to answer questions in a short, matter-of-fact manner and stop. The same is true of the sales call.

Principle #10: Notes Page

Principle #11: Never, Never, Never

Have you ever been rejected and asked why? Have you ever lost a sale and asked why? Have you ever been expecting something that was not delivered on time and asked why? Have you ever been oversold and underperformed and asked why? I am sure you have experienced all of the above at some time or another.

Did the answer to the *why* questions seem plausible? Did the answers appear to be the truth? Did you accept the answers at face value, or did you question them?

In a sales scenario where you are not the winner, not the chosen vendor, and you ask why, you will *never* be told the real reason. I emphasize *never*. Whatever you are told is the reason that your service or product was not chosen is NEVER, NEVER the actual reason. Please trust me on this. It is easy to accept the answer to the why and attempt to "fix" what is not really broken. You not only lose the sale but start down a rabbit hole that will further distract you from the actual reason and cost you time and additional lost sales.

Accept that the objection to your service or product is not real but a way for the buyer to move on in a less contentious manner—an easy and comfortable avenue for the buyer to take. When you hear the objection or reason you lost the sale, take the position that you know it is a deflection. Be savvy and know that there is an underlying reason that is not being shared with you. Is it price? Is it delivery time? Is it a quality issue? Is it a lack of customer service? Is it support after the sale? Believe me, none of these are *ever* the real issue.

I tried and tried to convince on of my prospects years ago to buy my service. I was told different reasons that my service was not as good as my competitor's. I was told it was price. I was told it was not as timely. The list went on and on. None of the objections were real. I later found out the reason. My competitor was dropping off a fifth of Jack Daniels to the buyer's home every Friday. I wasted time trying to offer better pricing, better timing, etc. I wasted time and effort (and the opportunity to sell to other prospects) trying to "fix" a problem that was not there. I was never going to make that sale.

I encountered a similar situation when I discovered my competitor was my prospect's brother-in-law. Do you think either buyer would have told me the real reason?

It is, therefore, better to dig deep into the unknown to find the real reason. Only then can you address the real issue and hopefully find a way to navigate your way around the hidden reason and secure a sale. *Never, never, never* take the reasons you are given as fact. It will save you a lot of precious time and energy.

Principle #11: Notes Page

Principle #12: Recycling

The sales call is usually a series of back-and-forth questions and answers. We have already discussed the effect of asking questions to get the prospect involved and talking (hopefully about themselves). After securing a clear understanding of the prospect's needs and expectations, it is time to move to a different method of question and answer as you move toward the close. The introductory round of questions was very open-ended, as the more feedback you receive, the better positioned you are to match needs to features.

As you narrow the conversation to close the sale, you must now move to "closed-ended" questions. Closed-ended questions are questions that can simply be answered with a "yes" or "no" or sometimes a "maybe." As you now have a clear understanding of your position regarding the prospect's needs, it is time to reinforce why your product or service is the best option. It is also time to reposition your competitors.

By "recycling," you can pinpoint the critical issues, address all the objections, and, as a residual benefit, automatically reposition the competition. So how does it work?

Example:

XYZ salesperson: "We have discussed several aspects of your buying decisions, and one very important point is price. If I can match or beat your current pricing or convince you that my proposal is a greater value, will you switch from ABC to XYZ?"

Buyer: "No, pricing is just one area in which I believe XYZ is behind ABC. Your product's warranty is not as good."

XYC salesperson: "OK, if I can offer you a better price or value and match or beat ABC's warrantee, will you switch to XYZ?"

Buyer: "Well, no. You see, your product's delivery time is lacking."

XYC salesperson: "I get it. If I can meet or beat your delivery time requirements, pricing, and warranty, do we have a deal?"

Buyer: "Well, maybe. I am still concerned about your installation protocol."

XYZ salesperson: "If I assure you that our installation will be personally supervised by me, and we meet all the other issues we have discussed, are you ready to switch to XYZ?"

Buyer: "Hm, you make a strong case to change to XYZ, but I'm really not sure I am ready to pull the trigger on the change."

XYZ salesperson: "I am a little confused. I have promised to address all your concerns. If there are no other issues, why would you not move forward and replace ABC with XYZ?"

ENTER THE TAKEAWAY

One of the most powerful sales tactics is the Takeaway.

This tactic takes the ultimate confidence. You must be prepared to lose the sale. The Takeaway is simply walking away, taking back all you had proposed and moving on to the next prospect.

Have you ever been to a car dealership to buy a car? You negotiate. The salesman will not meet your terms, so you stand up and leave. As you get about halfway to your car, here comes the salesperson, ready to accept your terms. This is the takeaway in reverse.

At one point in my sales career, I was selling residential real estate. I was representing the buyers, husband and wife. We contracted on a home, and the closing was thirty days out. During the first twenty days, I received at least three calls a day from the buyers (sometimes six or seven) to question every aspect of the home. They were not sure they should go through with the purchase. They kept asking more and more concessions from the seller. They were wearing out the seller and me. With ten days to go before closing, I finally decided it was time for the takeaway. When I received the buyers' next phone call to complain again, I said, "You know, I really don't think this house is for you. Let us terminate the contract and start searching for another home that you would feel more comfortable with." The buyers responded, "No, we really want *this* home." The phone calls pretty much stopped, and the buyers closed on the home.

You as the salesperson can walk away. If the prospect really wants to buy, he or she will come walking to you. You have nothing to lose. And many times, the buyer will agree to move forward with you. Give it a try.

Getting back to the XYZ salesman example:

Buyer (possible answer #1): "You know, you are right. You *have* addressed and satisfied my concerns. Where do I sign?"

XYX salesperson: "Great. I promise you will not regret this decision."

Buyer (possible answer #2): "I still cannot jump to XYZ. Your product is just not giving me the comfort level I have with ABC, so I am staying with ABC. Thank you for your time and effort, and best of luck moving forward."

XYZ salesperson: "And that's your final answer?"

Buyer: "I'm sorry, but it is."

Buyer's answer #1 speaks for itself. By recycling until all objections and issues have been satisfactorily addressed, the buyer had no reason left not to change to XYZ. And, as a residual benefit, the competitor was repositioned. By recycling, you closed the deal.

Buyer's answer #2 is a different but previously addressed dynamic. Remember *never, never, never*? You have addressed all the issues, needs, and requirements and satisfied the buyer's objections, only to be given a lame reason by the buyer. Red flag.

At this point, my mind goes straight to "it is not the *real* reason." The reason given obviously reflects the real reason, which has not been revealed. Now I know a lot about this buyer simply by his or her rejection without a plausible reason. The reason given is never, never, never the real deal. There is really nothing more to do at this point other than keep this buyer on your radar, as there is a good chance that the buyer will experience a situation that will require a change. In fact, the buyer will more than likely need to urgently correct a problem and will reach out to you, giving you a rock-solid opportunity to make a sale. If you had written off this buyer and not followed up, you would have wasted an opportunity.

Principle #12: Notes Page

Principle #13: Zip It

Sometimes a sales call is much easier than the recycling example, but a potentially solid sale can go south if you are not aware of the Zip It principle. Many times, sales professionals are so locked into the sales process that they miss the "sales signal." When the buyer sends a "sales signal," it is time to zip it or STOP TALKING, complete the needed paperwork, and close the deal.

It is common for sales professionals to keep selling once the buyer has been sold. It is important to be aware of subtle words or actions that imply the buyer is ready to buy and to shift to consummating the deal. The buyer may also expressly state that you have successfully made the sale. In either scenario, you must *stop selling*. You have done your job.

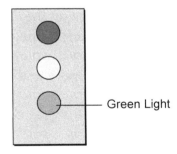

Green Light

What are some of the "buying signals" that indicate the buyer is ready to buy? Body language can be one.

The Buyer:

- Starts to relax
- Stops concentrating on the process
- Sits back
- Reaches for a pen
- Nods
- Puts hands in the temple position

Verbal signals:

- "OK, I like this."
- Asks questions that indicate the sale has been made
- Asks "when" questions
- Asks "where" questions
- Asks "how" questions

Express Signals:

- "Do you have the paperwork?"
- "Where do I sign?"
- "Good job. Let's do this."
- "OK, what is the next step?"
- "I'll have my people get the paperwork to you."
- "I look forward to making this work for both of us."
- Etc.

In any of these examples, *stop selling*. The *selling* portion of the process is over. Zip it and sign on the dotted line. There is still time to kill the deal if you keep selling. Do not make the mistake of continuing unnecessary discourse. It can only result in the buyers changing their minds based on something that is not agreeable to them.

Read the tea leaves. Finish closing the deal. And zip it!

Principle #13: Notes Page

Principle #14: Check Please!

Why do you work?

Why are you in business?

Why is the CLOSE important to you?

I will never forget my first day of a business class in college. The professor asked the question "What is the purpose of a business?" He stated there is only one answer: "To make money."

Making money is not evil. It does not involve taking advantage of anyone. It is the fuel that powers our capitalist economy. So go and make as much money as you possibly can.

Any venture that does not have a singular purpose, to make money, is not a business. It could be a hobby, or educational, or creative, etc.

Does your friend make and sell cookies because she enjoys it in business? No, she likes making cookies whether she makes money or not. I have a friend who makes and delivers sandwiches. She likes doing that. But she has no business plan and no concept of whether she is *making money* or not. So is this a business? No, she is just doing what she enjoys.

You are in the *business* of selling to provide for yourself and your family. If you did not make money, you would not spend your time selling.

Some espouse that, if you take care of your clients' needs and demonstrate that you can provide their "fix," the money will follow. Although there is much truth to this, money should always be an equal part of your approach, and you should always calculate your ROI (return on investment) as you decide how to approach each client.

If all or part of your income is commission-based, sometimes you must take into consideration "cutting" your commission to seal the deal. At some point, you will reach a level of compensation that does not equal the time and effort you are putting forth. It is OK to walk away. (Remember the take-away.) Move on to clients who respect you and your time and expertise.

Therefore, the more efficiently you *sell*, the more money you will make. The content of this book is designed to help you *sell* better. As is stated in the beginning of the book, *selling better* is the one thing to concentrate on.

By selling better, you will cash more checks, have more fun, improve your self-esteem, earn respect, and totally improve your life. Enjoy cashing those checks. You deserve it!

Principle #14: Notes Page

Principle #15: The Long and Winding Road

A shortcut is the longest distance between two points.

—Murphy's Law

When life seems like easy street, there is danger at your door.

—Grateful Dead

Your clients are your clients now, but for how long? Your clients were someone else's clients before you. You have competition that would like to take your clients away. So what is your plan to protect the relationship and trust you have built? As in most relationships, there will be ups and downs. Things will go wrong along the way. Your competition will always be ready to pounce. Your goal is to build a long-term, win-win relationship that is as close to bulletproof as possible.

John F. Kennedy once said, "What's mine is mine, and what's yours is negotiable." Getting what you want at the expense of your client is clearly antithetical to a long-term relationship. Win-win is the goal.

The least productive and most costly element of sales is constantly having to resale after your competitors have snagged your business. Here are some tips:

- Never let your guard down. Always be looking over your shoulder for unexpected repositioning by your competition.
- Make sure your relationship is win-win. Only win-win will stand the test of time. Win-lose or lose-win will always be a short-term scenario with short-term gains and long term losses.

Be cognizant and practice what I call the three Cs:

- Consistency. Trust is built with consistency. You cannot be a winner without consistency. Consistency builds accountability.

- Conformity. Change can cause a lack of trust. Trust is vital to relationships. Keep your product or service the way it was agreed upon. Only change when change is indicated and only after discussing with your client.

- Consideration. Be empathetic where possible. Your client will need your ear from time to time. Do not be a stranger. Keep on top of your clients' personal and professional situations. These are self-evident. Be considerate, be consistent, and maintain conformity in the ongoing delivery of your product or service and in your communication, follow-up, and customer service.

However, the road can be long and winding. It is filled with temptations to take shortcuts. Avoid the shortcuts. Stay the course. It will be winding. But if you follow the above-listed actions and conduct, the road will lead to a solid and profitable journey in the long run.

By staying the course, you will have earned the trust of your clients, and you now have "influence" over their behavior. Influence, not image, is the key to long-lasting success in most businesses. Influence must be treated as seriously as any other part of your long-term mission.

Hopefully, by earning the trust of your clients and building a strong relationship, you may become friends. Becoming friends creates a bonus for both you and your client. Now you both are truly trustworthy and open and honest in areas inside and outside of business.

My wife has a painting in our kitchen that reads, "The road to a friend's house is never long." If you and your client become friends, the road will be shorter and straighter.

Principle #15: Notes Page

Additional Principle: Turn the Tables

Let us discuss how these 15 Principles can work to your advantage when *you* are the buyer.

Now it's time for you to use the Principles outlined previously to your advantage as a buyer. Turn the tables to get the best deal in your purchases.

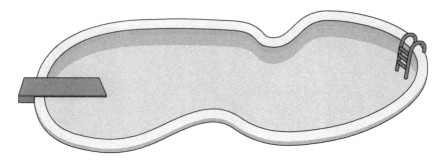

My wife, Ann, and I recently decided to add a swimming pool in our backyard. This was a major purchase and investment and required several vendors to complete the project. We started the process by interviewing swimming pool contractors to first decide what type of pool would work best for us. We looked at concrete (gummite), fiberglass, and vinyl. We picked fiberglass. Next, we interviewed several fiberglass pool companies. Using the Principles, we finally picked the company that checked the boxes and fit our psyche. Next, we had to interview and select a landscaping firm to fix the damage that would result from the installation of the pool. Next, we had to interview and select a company to provide pool-related furniture and equipment. Next was pool maintenance. And finally, we needed a stair rail from the deck down to the pool.

Ann and I reversed the Principles and selected companies that earned our trust and fit our psyche. These companies asked the right questions, determined our needs, made us feel important, and presented their products and services in a way that matched our expectations. Except one. The stair rail company.

We simply went online and found what we thought would work. We ordered it and contracted an installer to install it. It arrived, and guess what? It did not fit. We made the mistake of turning to the Internet instead of seeking knowledge from experts.

We then went back to interviewing local contractors, and we ended up with an awesome stair rail. So by using the Principles, we ended up with a successful outcome and a win-win. We wasted a lot of time and money trying to take a short-cut.

Use the 15 Principles in your buying decisions, and your outcomes will more than likely fit your expectations.

Notes Page

CLOSING STATEMENT

The 15 Principles will only help you get better if you implement them. There are many reasons not to act and to delay implementation, but there is power in the Principles. You will not perfect each Principle at first. Some will be easier and more comfortable. Some you will find difficult, and you will delay implementation due to fear of failure or simple procrastination. As you implement the more comfortable Principles, you will gain confidence in implementing the ones you find more challenging.

As you master the Principles, you will continue to find more success and the power and wisdom to change your world.

Remember, it all starts with the proper preparation and gaining the knowledge to power your approach. The value and urgency of your prospects should reflect where you spend your time and prioritize your daily schedule. It is important to understand what you are selling and to whom, and to identify the psychological "fix." Hold back the visuals, ask the right questions, get the prospect talking, and watch for buying signals. Be careful about volunteering info, and remember a rejection reason is not real. Recycle, close the deal, and cash your check!

Completing a successful sale is an art. Shallow and trendy advice rarely works. It takes a process. I hope the 15 Principles outlined in this book will support and complement your personal style and lead to more sales and more success.

ACKNOWLEDGEMENTS

When I decided to write this book, I knew it would take the support of my family, first and foremost. If not for the love and support of my wife, Ann, the book would not be what it is. Our children and grandchildren were just as helpful and added some new perspectives, as the world is changing.

I benefited from the lessons I learned and the mentorship of leaders like Stephen Deitch, Brenda Benson, David Nirshl, Bryan Maddex, Bob Labombard, Bill Melton, and others who tolerated me in many ways but were and are great role models.

My good friends John George, Wick Morse, Phil Heydt, Dick Gray, George Helms, Bob Lyborolopolis, Bob Maxson, Jack McCole, Joe Wilson, Todd Taylor, Paul Matthews, and many others that embraced my desire to write this book and kept encouraging me to the finish.

A special thanks to Stuart Ward (surprised), who taught me that business can be fun (remember Puerto Rico and the Doral Open?).

A special acknowledgement goes to my deceased father-in-law, Paul (Soapy) Glasener, who was the consummate business-man, the best salesman I have ever known, a great athlete, and a true inspiration to all who were fortunate to have known him.

Thanks to all who, along the way, taught and influenced me to be the best I could be in both my professional and personal life.

ABOUT THE AUTHOR

Throughout my business career, sales were the spark that motivated me the most. Whether I was working for a large corporation or my small businesses, sales were the part that I enjoyed the most. I have reinvented myself many times and have embraced the challenges of learning new businesses and the greatest challenge: starting my own companies. I love to teach the Principles outlined in this book. I love sports, especially golf, and I have accomplished the goal of playing golf in all fifty states. I am a big fan of my alma mater, the University of North Carolina at Chapel Hill, and follow and root for the Tar Heels. I am also a fan of our local pro teams, the Charlotte Hornets and the Carolina Panthers. I live with my wife, Ann, in Indian Land, South Carolina, but I can almost see my native North Carolina from my front door. We are proud parents of three sons, and they and their wives and our ten grandkids keep us terribly busy.

CPSIA information can be obtained
at www.ICGtesting.com
Printed in the USA
FSHW020001011021
85163FS

9 781638 379881